AF286085

Amilly Scoth

prom
queen

poetry

Impressum
Bibliografische Information der Deutschen Nationalbibliothek: Die Deutsche
Nationalbibliothek verzeichnet diese Publikation in der Deutschen Nationalbiblio-
grafie; detaillierte bibliografische Daten sind im Internet über dnb.dnb.de abrufbar.
Die automatisierte Analyse des Werkes, um daraus Informationen insbesondere
über Muster, Trends und Korrelationen gemäß §44b UrhG („Text und Data Mi-
ning") zu gewinnen, ist untersagt.
© 2024 Amilly Scoth
Herstellung und Verlag: BoD – Books on Demand, Norderstedt

ISBN 9783759758125
prom queen
the little screwed up poetry book
Scoth, Amilly
@amillyscoth
amillyscoth@gmail.com

for you

play

Icy Prom Queen

It was empty
I could hear every click of my heels
... click ...
... clack ...
... click ...
— silent screams — echoes —
In my sleep
Across the ballroom
It makes you
So icy & cool
Pearls are running of my body

On my own

You left
me there
I danced
alone here
To my own
heartbeat
You betrayed
me,
When I couldn't
see red
I still can
feel this
beat

Can I have this last dance?

And I regret
the look on
your face
I wish I could
resist
The day
I met the
color blue
I could've
run away from you

Now can I have this last dance,
Last chance to get away from your blues

Drive away

Like all these
trees
Drive away
Like
Past fading to memories

And all these me's
I tried to be
Passing away
Like
A train is leaving from the station

Will you be there?
When the past of mine fades
into memories of yours.
When they fade to grey as I grow older.
And it fits in my hair all too great.

Will we memorize?
All the stories we made.
When we were wildly & madly in love
Freely in love...

Block out

I just block them out of my life
Like a red button,
you avoid to push & pull

But not in my mind
Or my heart

Blue

I get a little bit blue
When I think of you
Thought you knew
The small things
about me
Thought I just knew
Your all too cool
Attitude
And I thought I knew
you
After all this time
I can't let go of it
I could've go back in time
And meet you again

Roses

Withered
Roses
Under
Covered
Ice
Sheets
&
A
Golden
Star
Shines
On
You
I glistened through your darkest grays

Someone better

I always thought
— I find someone better —
For myself

Break your heart again

I don't wanna break
Your heart
(again)
I just go
And find my darkest path
Without you

Waiting ... tick ... tick ... tick...

I've been
Waiting for you

... tick ... tick ... tick...

I've been longing
For something new

... tick ... tick ... tick...

Visit an empty room

to miss someone is to visit an empty room
Dark, Lonely, Sad.

self-reflection

It's a battle
To love
To live
Like I do
And watch it
...Mirror burns all the time...
When its all OK
And safe & sound
In your arms back again

Meet again

Makeup,
Parfume,
Red dress, like my lips
High heels on,
Fake smiles come along...,
All my so-called friends in a row
Meet some new under this disco ball

Do it again
            and
                    again.

Maybe I should rather have a table for one
than a second with ...

Mess in a dress

I always wanted
— searching for something new —
To be a mess in a dress not in my head

Always searched
to be a... a mess
In my dress
Instead of in my head

Buzzing

It keeps me buzzing
How drunk
I'm with you
I'm all over my blues
To let you know
I like the feeling of being with you on Sundays
                            with you on Sundays

Not drunk!

When I'm drunk
I pretend not to be
(But I'm head over heels)
I'm sure with it
I'm in you
Like I'm pretending not to be drunk

— When dawn meets dust
      I hold your hand tight in mine —
I said to you one afternoon

Rhymes

Changes my rhymes
All by myself
Just to fit in your long list of number ones
You want me to make your plan come true
Only to check
What stayed
away
from me

Don't you remember?!

What happened last July
Now in a dusty box of letters
Under my bed

Red dress

Bought this red dress to impress
Thought at this,
what a mess
I'm trying to become...
but it's all in my head
it won't get out
when I didn't let it be

Leaves

The best way to leave
is to play it fast
On someone new

Glistened night

Midnight stars,
Glistened nights
— glitch in the matrix —
It glistened all over me

Dancing along

Disco ball
Like an endless
Revolution
of you & me
Dancing along

Diamond ocean

Falling from the trees
Down to the ground
— sparkles peaceful
like a diamond ocean —
I'm going back into the woods
— wind in my sailing heart —
Never felt more alive
As leaves in the fall

Cruel endings

All the time
cruel endings
breaking through
the wall

Darkest smoke

It's windy in the air
— LOST —
See now
The darkest smoke
Creeping along the boat
I made for myself
to survive

Lost an enemy

Once upon a time
I lost an enemy
She was supposed to be a friend
Back in the good old days
Now I got stronger than she could ever be
Because she never lost something true

Hold onto you

Can't keep
Hold onto you
As long as you didn't do it for me too

When you were there
I could've held onto you too

Wiped Fingerprints

On these old guitars
On these frosted windows
On wet cement
Wiped fingerprints

Saw a realness

I saw a realness
In us
But it's gone
The time
You weren't with me

You saw a realness
In my eyes
An emptiness
In me
In my sleepless nights
Saw a realness in something that wasn't real

Sunshine mornings

Sunshine
Mornings
In my coffee
In your eyes

I never saw anything else than this

Never had a real friend

I never had a real friend
Like this
Never wanted more
Than you

Dancing when its pouring

Dancing when it's pouring
Seems to me
A real wild
Run
A long sleepless night

When you're out of breath

Dust & Dirt (on red dress)

Remember the poet
— The pen & paper —
He wrote about
a long coat
covering
this
red dress
buried alive in the deepest of winter
and when the snow thawed
it was all covered with
dust & dirt
& forgotten memories

Never found sunlight

Have never found sunlight
As long as
You couldn't get home to me

Short afternoon

A dusty gown
So old the time
lies in the aftermath
So long it seems
so short was the afternoon

Pictures - Frames - Memories

Twenty-two
And still recover
from our pass out l
                    o
          v
                e
only the pictures in frames
lie in memories

Couldn't remember it too well
What happened since our fallout

Crawled to my own grave

Crawled to my own grave
in the afternoon
It's hard to breathe
In a crowded room
For no one just me

Wrecked to the skin & bones
All in all in a nervous body
Crawled to my own grave in the afternoon
Buried in my own troubles
I made so proudly with agony

Prom Queen will be a dream fever

It's an illness
— I mess with it
all the damn time —
Prom Queen
will be a dream fever
forever and ever

Someone's hand

Someone's hand coming strong
Someone's holding on
Someone still keeps someone's hand in his own

People talking

People talking shit
People talking much
I don't get what they want from all the lies
they saying

Chasing mistakes

All I ever do is
chasing mistakes
And never getting
wiser
While they keep lying
about the truth

I'm buried alive with it

Liars never tell one truth

They'll never
Tell one simple truth
Liars will be liars
All over & over
again
they never tell one truth

Red lipstick & a red dress

Bloody lips,
Beating hearts,
One lipstick smudged on a red dress of their
own

Found one to catch

Never wanted anybody else
Found one to catch
And never wanted to give it away
Held on this heart of life
On the right side of your hand

The promise

It makes her laugh,
even if it's not for long
the biggest promise of all time

Cold hands hold a cold heart

So cold
It hurts
No more
Warmth
Will (n)ever get through
anymore

That's when I feel truly me

Remember the flooding blood

Came flowing out of nowhere
Too far
Away
From my last dance
with you
just remember the flooding blood
in my dreams
made of dust

They wear high heels

Highest pressures
Climbing on the most elevated
standards

I'm coming through
And show you the prove

please, press play

Turns in memories,
And claims frequencies,

— In a second
Song
please, press play —
The forgotten laughter.

It's one-way-around
please, press play

Face in my hands

Hiding with my hands in my face.
I'm no one and nowhere to find

— Rebels...
....Minds...
...Keep holding me high —

A vagabond by heart

I'm never going away
and
turning back
I just hold my face in my hands

Mascara black

As black as my coffee
when it's the last hope

You know mascara black eyes
Without a doubt
In your beautiful view
good-for-nothing,
Needed a lot
And
All the way
I couldn't find...

You know I'm a vagabond
To be found someday

Losing puzzle piece

Trying to remember
Laying down
On the ground
Last puzzle piece
Slip through my fingers

The artistic
way goes along
bit by bit

It's the state of mind
that loses the last puzzle piece

Never found why?

Still walking by
Never found why?
I should be.
Finding a reason someday...
to stay
— Why? —

The reason slips through my hands

One reason was enough
Can't find one again
It all slips
Through my hands
Like water
In the Atlantic
Am I drowning?

Could've walked away

Could've walked away
If I never held on to something

Trying to recover

Twenty-something
And still growing up
I'm just trying
to recover
from my teens
I lost on my eighteenth
birthday

Tired of smiling

Tied my hair
Tired all the time
Don't know why I'm running
Like a kid
when I'm still a kid
Couldn't match the others with their lipstick
smiles
Formed something new
— didn't know what it is —
Could've remembered what it was
Should've known it all the time
Lost the hair tie
And the shoes
Hanging from the edge like prom queens
shouldn't do

Shaking hands

Shaking hands
& beating hearts

Sometimes a crier
with shaking knees

Heartless crier

A cold heartless
crier
is cruelty to the bones

Catch the Prom Queen
And you'll find out

We all live in a game
        called chess
We all want to win
and never to lose

Writing a letter to someone someday

Changed the subjects
Everyday
Now I am writing letters
one after another
Can't keep
my mind away from one question
— Too stuck in a world of my own —

It's my escape
To switch it on
The mayhem-mode of my brain
Someday
I'm asking you to stay!

stop

the little screwed up poetry book

Amilly Scoth

to
myself

don't be so hard on yourself
someday your day will come

this is the thing

football shirt no. 5

theater blvd

spaces between

behind my back

eyes are my arrows

scattered mind

split opinion

universal eye

lost in letters

heartstrings

messed up

showdown

a life in metaphors

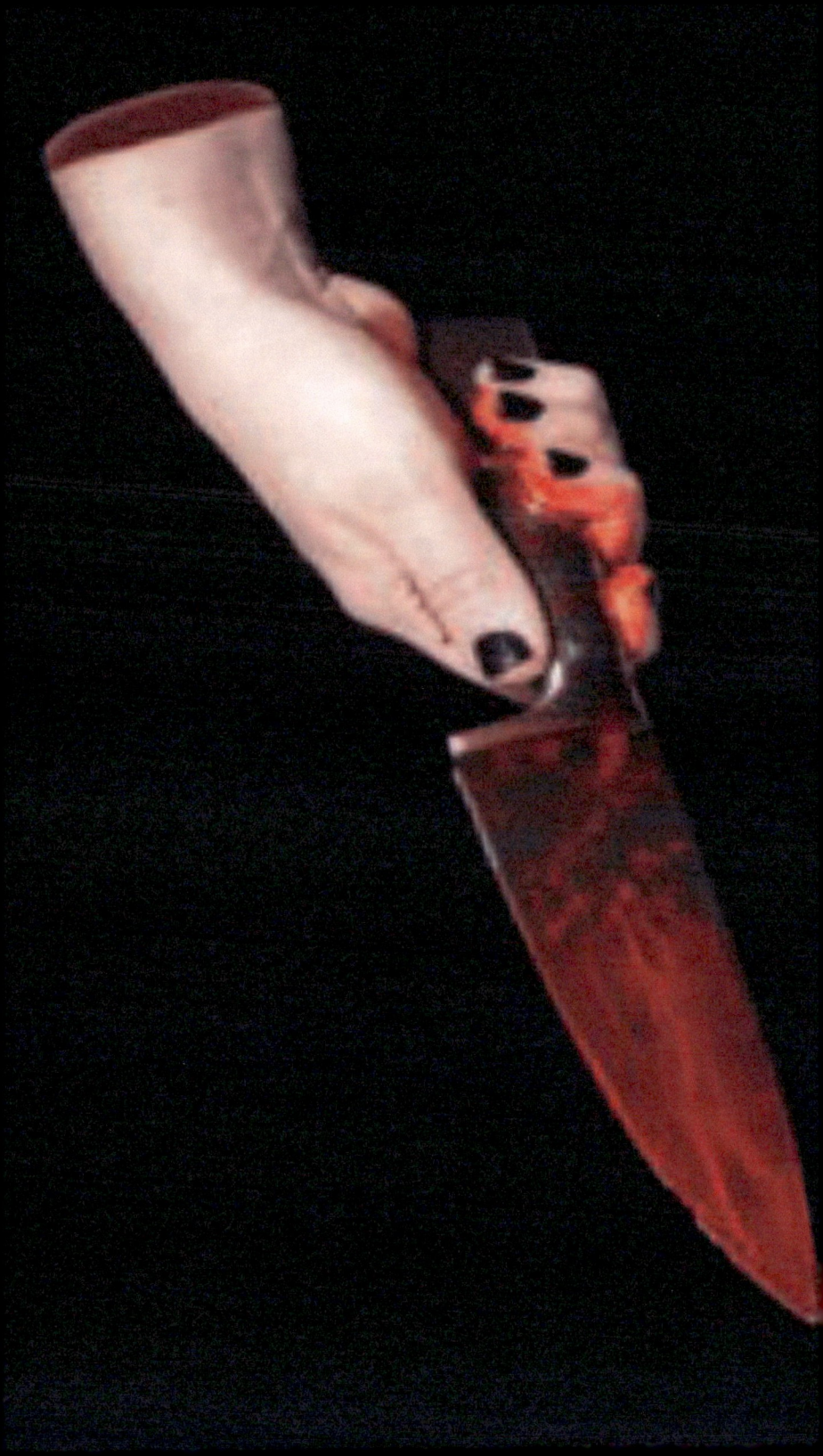

this is the thing

This is the thing to pretend
when nothing is right or wrong
people move away,
yeah, this is the thing

What's worth dying or living for
if you can't
stop them from thinking

Why are you trying
so hard, baby
if you can't put it together
or apart

When the walls are
crumbling down and everything
is dragging you to the ground
Why are you still here
and running like a wild child

I bet someday
it's your time to roll
and ride away
like a cowboy into the wind
it'll be right for you
just hold your breath a little
longer and move on

football shirt no. 5

Everyone leaves
like ghosts
cause fall is short,
and winter is so long

It's always a last goodbye
rain came pouring down
- motionless on the ground -

Left the football shirt no. 5
in a box under the bed
Where we used to put
our dreams in

Am I fine to leave it all behind?
Is it okay to choose
the other way around?

And beyond every journeys end
I'll stay
if you ask

theater blvd

clock ticking
people talking
cassettes on repeat

burned out playlist of
— sinners in heaven—

close your eyes
when it's all too bright
the show is ending
soon
on theater blvd

but never repent
the things you've done
unless it's all yours in the end

it'll be gone
in the next
few minutes

spaces between

couldn't break the walls
wouldn't take the calls
they were lost on me

- found the tiniest of covering -
a room to rest my bones
wandered lonesome
back and forth
all I have are spaces between

going along
through the old grey house
finding the devil
in the middle
- and out of reach -
- and out of mind -
- and out of breath -

I'm on the run
in circles
can't stop misrecollecting
about us

all I got are spaces between

behind my back

Do I still have
ten minutes to sleep?
Where are you, you
left nothing to say
scrawled „the name" on my hands
Where's my other half?

I think I crawl backwards,
backwards in the right direction

and these voices
keep me up at nights
What if you were here?
What would you do now?

behind my back
there is much to take
Arrows!!!
they throw at me

And fire,
I'm like a witch on the pyre

scream as loud as you can
no one can hear it
when you're alone
in a crowded room

eyes are my arrows

- spreading out -
always seeing red
when it's blue

- burning out -
I'm better undercover
when the lights go on

my hopes are high
to meet you someday
I dream of you all the damn time

good things will happen again
lights keep me searching
for someone better
to find my soul

I bet my eyes are my arrows
when you look in my direction

scattered mind

the second day & it's all damaged
in the writing
it's addressed to hell

my hands are trembling
on this torn out paper

you wrote last night
just in time my scattered mind
is shattering all over myself

but the caves and cliffs
are too high, - out of reach -
I couldn't lean on
the waves are too strong

it's not in me to be recollect
or be replaced
what was never mine
will never be yours

I'm standing here alone
to be hypnotized by something
it couldn't be me,
no,
no matter how
- it's all I have now-

split opinion

don't talk
don't give your mind away

the chances
you think about me
are zero to none
when we didn't even meet

what would've been
if we'd lasted

don't give the chances
to lose opinions about me
and think it out loud
with somebody else

it's my greatest talent
to ruin what you're thinking
but maybe someday
you'll understand
the split opinion too

maybe we're all the same
with different tattoos
on our skins
and disparate chances
to reach our dreams

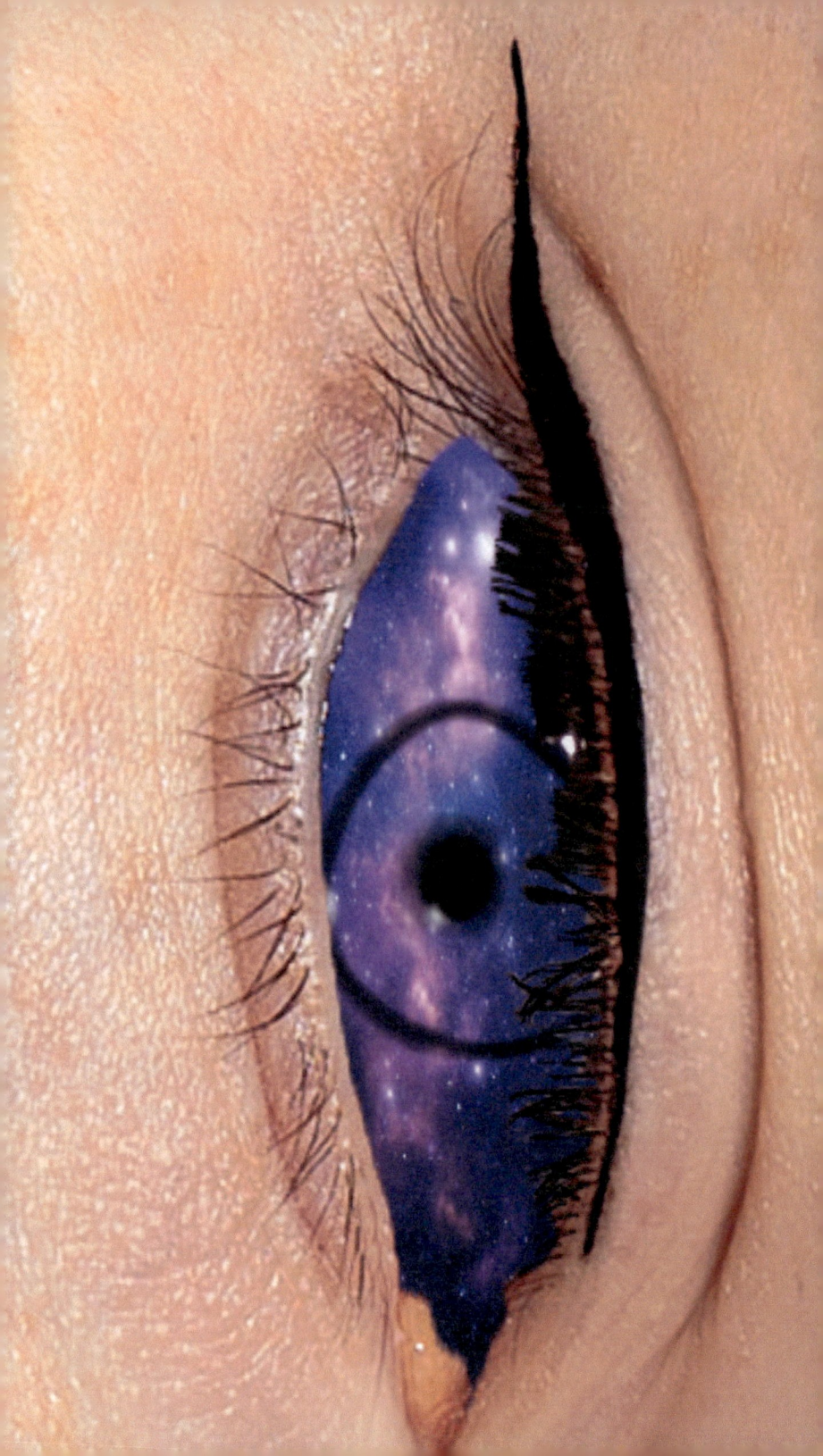

universal eye

can't see it clear
can't catch a star
I'm starstruck
by the bright side

who I do want to impress
when I'm going out
just feeling like a mess
I'm saying out loud

it seems so nice
it's all in the universal eye
make me believe
something is real

lost in letters

What does it mean
to be closed in books
and locked in cages
like a wild bird in captivity?

and all they ask for is
— a penny for your thoughts —
but what does it cost

by hook or by crook
I'm lost in letters
can't tell otherwise
I'm zoning out

a wild flower turning red
and entrancing all of you
I just had my time to grow
I'm flying around
above all of you now

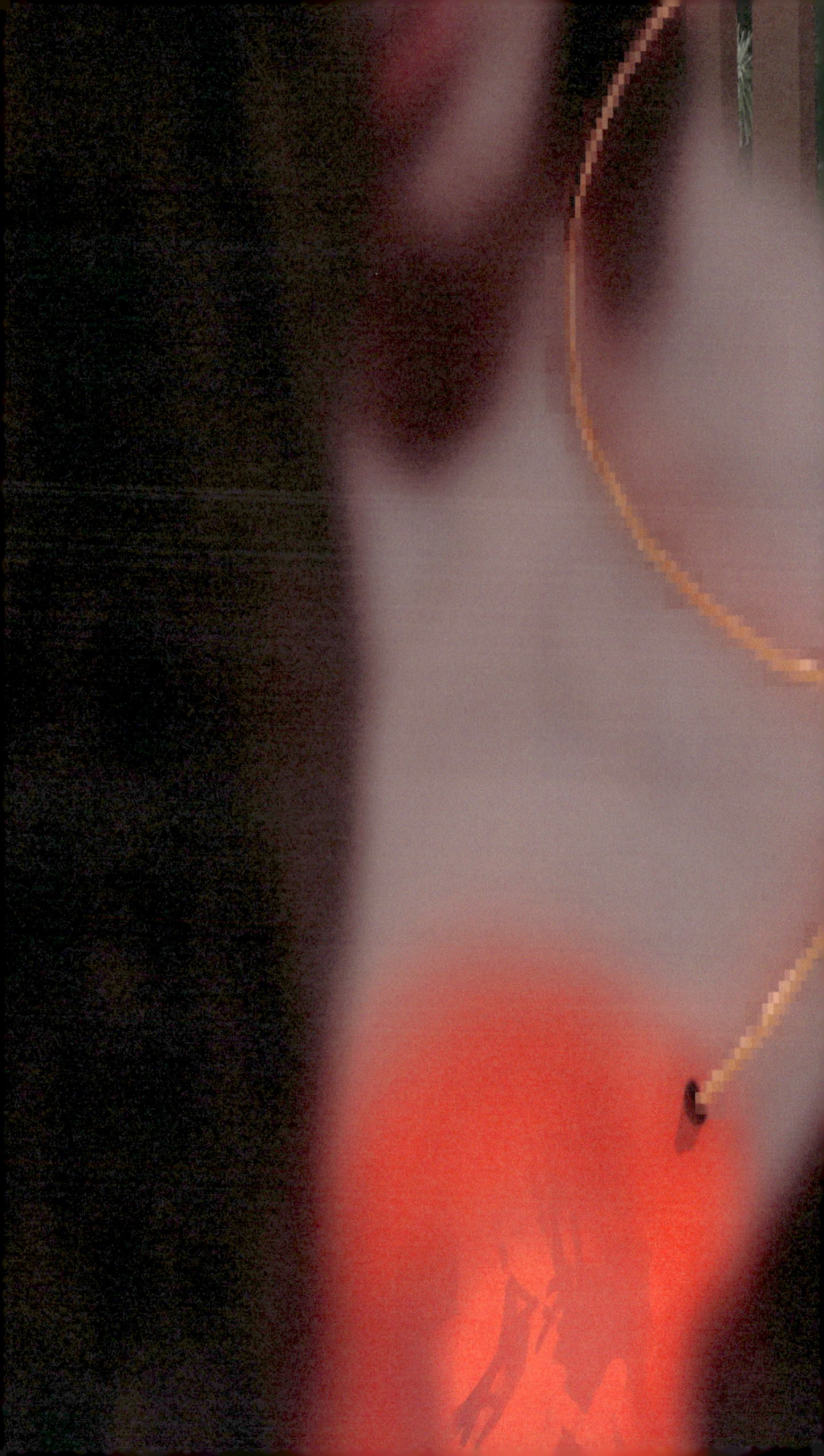

heartstrings

and I say to you
the second cord always breaks
twice as good
as the first

never made
the right decision
on the most wrong path
it's as long as the road

the reasons to be
someone you wanted
for so long
it's only in your blood
flowed through it
in waters

be a ghost
or be ghosted
does it matter now?
just let it go

the ghost in me
pulls the strings
that my heart
needs to live

messed up (in the head)

I believe it was
a Monday morning
when you said
I'm burned & lost inside my mind
(you'd be still on my mind)

I'm a catastrophic thinker,
- classic anchor -
out of time
& out of line

I'm a little messed up,
stressed out
in my mind
I'm a little messed up,
stressed out
along the roads

Damn, it's creeping up on me,
keeping me down
thinking about these
fucking situations
Now I'm a little stressed out
when I look into your eyes

A little messed up
it comes back to me
in blues
but since
I saw you for the first time,
it spins faster,
and it'll never stop
„Maybe all I ever be
is a one-girl-band
so i can be free"

I'm a little messed up,
while I drift away
to hide the part
where you hit me the most
because you said
I'm a little messed up,
a little messed up,
messed up

Like you too!

showdown

I just want to be heard
by no one
just anybody
cause I have a voice

— someday —
I say to myself
no matter by whom
when all the curtains are closed

the sooner you let down yours
the higher the chances
to win

this must be done
with broken
glasses
and a little bit of a lonely heart

my showdown is coming soon

a life in metaphors

In the end,
we all have metaphors
and rainy days
It might be done
and nothing will be unsaid

it means so much
to live a life in metaphors

I'm mesmerized
by all these strange
conversations
and mindless consequences

I regret the day
when I broke
your heart
never got over it
that's the prize
to live a life in metaphors

Thank you